Happy Birthday

love
cousin
Florence
2009

snapshot·picture·library

AIRPLANES

snapshot • picture • library

AIRPLANES

FOG CITY PRESS

Published by Fog City Press,
a division of Weldon Owen Inc.
415 Jackson Street
San Francisco, CA 94111 USA
www.weldonowen.com

WELDON OWEN inc.
Executive Chairman, Weldon Owen Group John Owen
President, CEO Terry Newell
Senior VP, International Sales Stuart Laurence
VP, Sales and New Business Development Amy Kaneko
VP, Publisher Roger Shaw
VP, Creative Director Gaye Allen
Executive Editor Elizabeth Dougherty
Assistant Editor Sarah Gurman
Art Director William Mack
Production Director Chris Hemesath
Production Manager Michelle Duggan
Color Manager Teri Bell

A WELDON OWEN production
© 2008 Weldon Owen Inc.

Library of Congress Control Number: 2008935244

ISBN-13: 978-1-74089-854-6

10 9 8 7 6 5 4 3 2 1

Color separations by Sang Choy International, Singapore.
Printed by Tien Wah Press in Singapore.

Have you ever flown in an airplane? Planes are amazing machines that fly all over the world. They often make short flights between cities, but they can also take you over oceans to other countries far away.

If you live near a busy airport you might see airplanes flying through the sky all the time. Do you have a favorite kind of airplane?

At the airport, planes line up at gates where passengers get on or off.

Ground crews
fuel the planes,
clean them, and
repair them
if needed.

Passengers climb the steps to
get onboard. Their luggage
is loaded separately.

Some planes are loaded with cargo at the front and others at the back.

The pilot sits
on the left side
of the cockpit.
The copilot is
on the right.

The plane speeds along the runway and then up, up, and away!

Airplanes fly thousands of feet above land and water. Sometimes, when you look out the window, all you can see are clouds.

Planes fly around the clock—from very early in the morning to late at night.

Airplanes can take you almost anywhere!

The decorations on a plane tell you many things. Look at the tail of this plane. Where do you think it came from?

These planes are from different countries. Their tails look like their national flags.

Other planes
are decorated
with pictures
of birds.

When a plane
takes off or lands,
it must line up
with the runway.

Not all planes land on the ground. Float planes can land on water!

This small business jet holds only a few people. It can land at small airports where big jets can't.

Some planes
use propellers.
Their blades
spin around
very fast.

Most jets have one or two engines on each wing. Some even have an engine on the tail!

Gliders don't have engines. They're pulled into the sky by another plane.

The double-decker Airbus A380 is the biggest passenger airplane in the world! It has four powerful engines to help it fly.

But the 747 is still the best-known jumbo jet.

This cargo plane carries packages, not people. Did you notice that the only windows are in the cockpit?

Some planes have other jobs to do. This plane drops water onto forest fires to help put them out.

Other planes perform fantastic stunts in the sky, called aerobatics.

Some planes fly in groups. The smoke from these planes is drawing the colors of the Italian flag.

These pilots
are showing
off their planes
at air shows.

People like
to watch
planes racing
against one
another, too.

When are you
flying off on your
next big adventure?

Boeing 737

The narrow-body (single-aisle) Boeing 737 is the best-selling commercial passenger jet ever. Airlines around the world use it for short- to medium-distance flights.

Airbus A320

The narrow-body (single-aisle) Airbus A320, used for short- to medium-distance flights, is the second best-selling commercial passenger jet. The 737 is first.

Boeing 747

The wide body (two aisles) of the 747 made it the first ever jumbo jet. The double-deck section in the front of the plane is used for either cargo or extra seating.

Airbus A380

The largest passenger airliner in the world today, the Airbus A380 has two full-length decks, two aisles, and 220 cabin windows. It typically seats 525 people.

Turboprop

Turboprop airplanes, like this Bombardier Dash 8, are powered by propellers. Turboprops use less fuel and can use shorter runways than similar-size jets.

Cargo plane

Cargo planes, such as this Airbus A310, carry goods—instead of passengers—long distances. They have large doors to make loading and unloading easier.

Business jet

Business or executive jets, like this Learjet 60, are used by companies to fly employees as an alternative to airline flights. These jets can fly into small airports, too.

Airtanker

Airtankers or "water bombers," such as this Antonov An-32p, fight forest fires. Crews fill the tanker with water at a base, or the pilot scoops it from a lake.

Float plane

Float planes, like this DHC-3-T Turbo-Otter, take off and land on water. Also known as seaplanes, float planes have large floats instead of wheels.

Aerobatic plane

Aerobatic planes perform stunts, such as loops and rollovers, in the air. They may leave colorful smoke trails behind, like these Stearman biplanes.

Glider

Gliders, like this Swift S-1, do not have engines. Powered planes tow gliders aloft, then release them to soar for hours on wind currents before gently landing.

Racing plane

Racing planes are light, agile, and very fast. The Edge 540, pictured here, is a popular race plane. Airplane races are held all over the world.

ACKNOWLEDGMENTS

Weldon Owen would like to thank the staff at Toucan Books Ltd, London, for their assistance in the production of this book: Ellen Dupont, managing director; Stefanie Smith, author and researcher; Vivian Foster, designer; and especially Hannah Bowen, project manager.